TILLS™

TEST OF INTEGRATED LANGUAGE & LITERACY SKILLS™

I0644944

Quick Start Guide

OVERVIEW

The Test of Integrated Language and Literacy Skills™ (TILLS™) tests oral and written language skills of school-age students age 6–18 years. The TILLS is a standardized, norm-referenced test validated for the following three purposes:

1. **To identify language and literacy disorders**
2. **To document patterns of relative strengths and weaknesses**
3. **To track changes in language and literacy skills over time**

The TILLS model is unique because its 15 subtests collectively measure skills at two language levels (sound/word and sentence/discourse levels) across oral and written language modalities (listening, speaking, reading, and writing). The model is described in Table 1.1 and Figure 1.1 in the *TILLS Examiner's Manual.* The TILLS subtests are curriculum-relevant because they reflect the language demands of curricula in Grades 1–12.

ADMINISTRATION

- **Time required:** Most students can complete all 15 TILLS subtests in a single 70- to 90-minute session with an experienced examiner. Less time is required if fewer subtests are administered. Subtests can be given in more than one session, provided testing is extended over no more than 4 weeks and rules are followed to keep administration of some subtests together (see Table 2.2 in the *Examiner's Manual*).
- **Test environment:** The testing environment should be positive, friendly, and welcoming. Examiners should provide a general introduction before beginning, such as "Most of these activities will seem like things you do in school. You will not get a grade, but it is important for you to do your best work. Some of the tasks may seem easy, and some may seem hard. It is okay not to know all the answers." For a younger student, you might add, "This test was designed to be hard enough for students all the way through high school, so don't feel discouraged if some parts seem hard."
- **Prompts and probes:** Examiners should encourage students with neutral prompts that do not convey specific feedback about the response correctness. For example, "You are doing a nice job," or "Good working." You may use limited probes for certain subtests (see specific subtest directions).
- **Oral instructions:** Standardized oral instructions for the examiner are presented in the *TILLS Examiner Record Form* using the following formatting: ***"quotation marks and bold italics."*** Read these directions in a conversational tone at a normal rate of speech and loudness. Instructions may be repeated as necessary, and coaching may be used only during the practice items for each subtest. Beyond that point, you must follow the specific instructions for each subtest outlined in the *Examiner's Manual.*
- **Feedback:** Examiners should ensure that students cannot see the *Examiner Record Form.* Mark every response (right or wrong) on the *Examiner Record Form* so that students cannot gather cues regarding the correctness of their responses.
- **Start points:** Examiners will see an arrow to the left of items where students of a particular age should begin testing. For example, "6–11" within an arrow indicates the point where students who are 6 through 11 years old should start. If there is an age-defined start point, use it. The exceptions are if a student has an intellectual disability that suggests a need to begin with Item 1 or if the examiner suspects a reading decoding problem that requires screening with Story 1 prior to the Reading Comprehension (RC) subtest. Instructions for each subtest are included on the *Examiner Record Form.*
- **Basals:** Basal rules are only relevant when the student is at an age that requires starting a subtest at a level higher than Item 1. When this occurs, it is essential to follow basal rules correctly so that the student's score on the subtest can be compared to the TILLS normative data. (For more information on basals, see pages 16–18 in the *Examiner's Manual.*)

  General instructions for basals: When establishing a basal score, if the student does not meet the criterion for basal when testing forward from any start point above Item 1, test backward from the first item administered until you establish the basal or administer Item 1. If you administer all items back to Item 1 without meeting the criterion for basal, testing *should be continued* by testing forward from the highest item previously administered until the ceiling criterion is reached or until all items have been administered. Any unadministered items preceding an established basal should be given a score of 1. If a student is at an age to start any subtest with Item 1, it is not necessary to establish a basal.
- **Ceilings:** Ceiling rules are used to establish when it is safe to stop testing because there is a high probability that the student will miss any higher numbered items. It is equally as important to establish ceilings correctly as it is for basals. Stopping prematurely can invalidate the subtest score.

  General instructions for ceilings: Follow the ceiling rules for each subtest to know when to stop testing. Be careful not to stop administering items until the student has met the criterion for the ceiling rule for the subtest. If you do administer items past the student's ceiling item, then give those items a score of 0 (even if the student answered correctly). (For more information on ceilings, see pages 17–18 in the *Examiner's Manual.*)

  A Note about Basals and Ceilings: Basal and ceiling rules vary by subtest. Those rules are on the *Examiner Record Form,* on the inside pages of this *Quick Start Guide,* and described in full in Chapter 2 of the *Examiner's Manual.* The *TILLS Examiner's Practice Workbook* also helps with practice in establishing basals and ceilings.

The *Examiner's Manual* provides a brief description of each subtest in Chapter 1 (pages 5–9) and complete instructions for administering are in Chapter 2.

SUBTEST 1: Vocabulary Awareness (VA)

Purpose: This subtest assesses a student's lexical knowledge, awareness of semantic relationships, and cognitive-linguistic flexibility.

Use as a stand-alone measure: Yes
Average time to administer: 15 minutes
Materials: *Examiner Record Form* (pp. 2–4), *Stimulus Book* (pp. 3–55)
Start rule: Start points for age ranges are indicated by arrows
Basal rule: 4 consecutive scores of 2 (both parts of each item must be correct)
Ceiling rule: 6 scores of 0 within a sequence of 8 consecutive items (both pairs must be incorrect on 6 out of 8 items)
Repetition: Allowed
Probes: Yes (as specified in the *Examiner's Manual*)

Special instructions:

- ***You may*** ask what two words mean if the student says they "mean the same."
- ***You may*** remind the student to tell how words go together based on what they mean, not how they are spelled.
- ***You may*** remind the student that the two words in a pair must go together in a way the third one does not.
- ***Do not*** provide definitions of words.
- ***Do not*** probe for more after an inadequate answer.

SUBTEST 2: Phonemic Awareness (PA)

Purpose: This subtest assesses the student's awareness of the individual speech sounds of language (phonemes).

Use as a stand-alone measure: Yes
Average time to administer: 3 minutes
Materials: *Examiner Record Form* (pp. 5–6), audio recording device (recommended)
Start rule: Start points for age ranges are indicated by arrows
Basal rule: 6 consecutive scores of 1
Ceiling rule: Scores 0 on 6 out of 8 consecutive items
Repetition: No (unless ambient noise interferes)
Probes: None

Special instructions:

- ***Do not*** draw attention to spelling or letters during coaching; use the word "sound" or "sounds."
- ***Do not*** name the initial sounds for the two practice items.
- ***Do not*** remind the student to remove only the first sound if the student reverts to a pattern of removing the full initial consonant cluster (e.g., *tr-* or *fl-*) during testing.
- If the student uses a consistent pattern of misarticulation associated with a regional or social dialect, ***do not*** penalize the substituted sound and give credit.

SUBTEST 3: Story Retelling (SR)

Purpose: This subtest assesses the student's ability to listen to, comprehend, and retell a story. This subtest can provide insight into a student's knowledge of narrative discourse structure.

Use as a stand-alone measure: Yes
Average time to administer: 4 minutes
Materials: *Examiner Record Form* (pp. 7–10), audio recording device (recommended)
  Story A: "Tommy the Trickster" for ages 6;0–11;11 (p. 7 of the *Examiner Record Form*)
  Story B: "The Rubber Raft" for ages 12;0–18;11 (p. 9 of the *Examiner Record Form*)
Start rule: Arrows with age ranges in years indicate which story to administer
Basal rule: None
Ceiling rule: None
Repetition: No (unless ambient noise interferes)
Probes: Yes (as specified in the *Examiner's Manual* and below)
Special instructions:

- ***Be sure*** to select the correct story for the student's age.
- You may probe for initiation by saying, ***"Just tell me anything you remember."***
- ***You may*** probe for completion by asking, ***"Can you think of anything more?"***
- No other probes are allowed during retelling.
- ***Do not forget*** to ask the four comprehension questions after the initial story retelling is complete.

SUBTEST 4: Nonword Repetition (NWRep)

Purpose: This subtest assesses a student's speech perception, the ability to hold a sequence of speech sounds in immediate memory, and the ability to reproduce those speech-sound (phonological) sequences accurately (without penalizing consistent articulatory substitutions).

Use as a stand-alone measure: Yes
Average time to administer: 4 minutes
Materials: *Examiner Record Form* (pp. 11–12), audio player, *Digital Audio Files* (Tracks 2–28), audio recording device (recommended)
Start rule: Start at the beginning for all students
Basal rule: None
Ceiling rule: Scores 0 on 6 out of 8 consecutive items
Repetition: No (unless ambient noise interferes)
Probes: None
Special instructions:

- ***Do not*** penalize dialectical differences or consistent articulatory substitutions.
- Use a digital audio player with quality speakers and adjustable volume.

SUBTEST 5: Nonword Spelling (NWSpell)

Purpose: This subtest assesses a student's ability to represent phonemic and morphemic components of novel words with conventional orthographic patterns. Using nonwords reduces the effect of experience and memorization of real words.

Use as a stand-alone measure: No (Subtest 4 must be administered immediately prior to Subtest 5 and in the same session.)
Average time to administer: 6 minutes
Materials: *Examiner Record Form* (pp. 13–14), *Student Response Form* (p. 2), pencil with eraser, audio player, *Digital Audio Files* (Tracks 29–55)
Start rule: Start at the beginning for all students (Do not administer to children age 6;0–6;5.)
Basal rule: None
Ceiling rule: Scores 0 on 6 out of 8 consecutive items
Repetition: No (unless ambient noise interferes)
Probes: None

SCORING AND INTERPRETING

The *Examiner Record Form* provides convenient formats (with instructions) for summarizing and interpreting TILLS scores for its three purposes of identifying language and literacy disorders, profiling patterns of strengths and weaknesses, and tracking changes over time (or use the *TILLS Easy-Score*™ tool to assist in this process). Use the **Scoring Chart** on the front cover of the *Examiner Record Form* (see the example depicted in Figure 1) to summarize the student's raw scores, transform them to standard scores, and create composites that will be used for interpreting the TILLS results. Use the **Identification Chart** (on page 39 of the *Examiner Record Form,* depicted in Figure 2) to identify language and literacy disorders. Use the **Profile Chart** and **Confidence Interval Charts** (on page 40 of the *Examiner Record Form,* depicted in Figures 3 and 4) to describe patterns of strengths and weaknesses. Use the **Tracking Chart** (on page 39 of the *Examiner Record Form,* depicted in Figure 5) to track changes in language and literacy skills over time. Examples are used in this section for a hypothetical 8-year-old girl to illustrate how to interpret TILLS scores for these purposes.

Using the Scoring Chart to Transform TILLS Subtest Scores to Standard Scores

You should always use standard scores or percentile ranks (never raw scores) when reporting TILLS results. Standard scores are based on a standardized relationship between the score obtained by the student and the normative distribution. TILLS subtest standard scores are scaled with a mean of 10 and a standard deviation of 3. TILLS composite standard scores are scaled with a mean of 100 and a standard deviation of 15. Percentile ranks reflect the percentage of students of the same age as the student tested who received a lower score than the one earned by that student.

Follow Steps 1 and 2 (printed on the Scoring Chart on the *Examiner Record Form* front cover) to transform raw scores to subtest standard scores and percentile ranks. For ❶, enter the raw scores for all subtests administered. For ❷, look up the Subtest Standard Scores and Percentile Ranks for the student's age in the *Examiner's Manual* Appendix. Enter them in the Subtest Scores section on the Scoring Chart.

	Subtest Scores and TILLS Total			Composite of Subtest Standard Scores				Identification Core Scores		
Subtest	❶ Raw Score	Standard Score and TILLS Total ❷	Percentile Rank	Sound/Word Composite Score	Sentence/Discourse Composite Score ❸	Oral Composite Score	Written Composite Score	Identification Core for 6- to 7-year-olds	Identification Core for 8- to 11-year-olds ❹	Identification Core for 12- to 18-year-olds
1 VA	25	9	42		9	9			9	
2 PA	5	3	2	3		3				
3 SR	23	11	47		11	11				
4 NWRep	15	5	5	5		5				
5 NWSpell*	2	6	4	6			6		6	
6 LC	16	10	40		10	10				
7 RC*	0	0	0		0		0			
8 FD	8	8	19		8	8				
9 DSR	22	11	49		11	11				
10 NWRead*	0	2	0	2			2		2	
11 RF*	47	0	0	0			0			
12a WE-Disc*	30	4	4		4		4		4	
12b WE-Sent*	1.00	7	3		7		7			
12c WE-Word*	96	11	50	11			11			
13 SC	9	13	75		13	13				
14 DSF	3	6	1			6				
15 DSB	0	6	0			6				
❺ Sum of the Subtest Standard Scores		112		27	73	82	30		21	
❻ Standard Scores of the TILLS Total and Composites		68		59	83	85	57		66	
Percentile Ranks for the TILLS Total and Composites		3		0	11	13	1		2	

Figure 1. Scoring Chart completed for an 8-year-old girl.

Using the Scoring Chart to Calculate TILLS Composites Scores

Follow Steps 3 through 6 (see Figure 1) using the Scoring Chart to enter the standard scores that make up each composite score, calculate the totals, and transform these totals to standard scores. The composites include the TILLS Total score (based on the column labeled Standard Score in Figure 1); four TILLS composite scores (Sound/Word, Sentence/Discourse, Oral, and Written); and one of three possible Identification Core scores to match the student's age. The Sound/Word and Sentence/Discourse composites are consistent with the language levels of the TILLS test model and are supported by scientific evidence from factor analysis in TILLS standardization research. The Oral and Written composites can be used to identify relative strengths and weaknesses in either modality. See Purpose 2 (on the back panel) for information on interpreting these composite scores.

For ❸, copy the standard scores into the open white cells in the same rows in any of the composites where they apply. For ❹, copy the standard scores into the open white cells in the column that matches the student's age. For ❺, calculate the sum of standard scores in any of the columns for which complete data are entered (you cannot calculate a composite score if any of the component subtests were not administered, except in the case of the TILLS Total for students 6;0-6;5 when the five subtests that are marked with an asterisk on the *Examiner Record Form* are not given). For ❻, look up the Standard Score and Percentile Rank for the Total TILLS score, any of the four Composite scores, and the Identification Core score in the age-related tables in the Appendix of the *TILLS Examiner's Manual* and enter them in the bottom two rows of the Scoring Chart.

Using the TILLS for Purpose 1: To Identify Language and Literacy Disorders

Identification Core scores are used to determine whether a student's TILLS results are consistent with the presence of a language/literacy disorder. The TILLS subtests that make up the Identification Core differ by age range, as seen in the variation in the open white cells in the three Identification Core score columns on page 1 of the *Examiner Record Form.* This reflects the fact that school-age students move through different phases of language learning as they progress through school, especially with regard to literacy.

- For 6–7-years-olds, the Identification Core includes Vocabulary Awareness (VA), Phonemic Awareness (PA), and Nonword Repetition (NWRep).
- For 8–11-year-olds, the Identification Core is made up of Vocabulary Awareness (VA), Nonword Spelling (NWSpell), Nonword Reading (NWRead), and Written Expression–Discourse Score (WE-Disc).
- For 12–18-year-olds, the Identification Core includes Phonemic Awareness (PA), Nonword Spelling (NWSpell), Reading Comprehension (RC), Reading Fluency (RF), and Written Expression–Word Score (WE-Word).

To use the Identification Chart on page 39 of the *Examiner Record Form* to decide whether a student's TILLS performance meets the criterion for identifying a language/literacy disorder, you must use the Sum of the Subtest Standard Scores (not the standard score) for the student's age-appropriate Identification Core. Use the following steps to interpret TILLS scores for the purpose of identifying language/literacy disorder.

❶ Copy the Sum of the Subtest Standard Scores from the age-appropriate column in the Identification Core Score section from the Scoring Chart on page 1 of the *Examiner Record Form* and enter it in the column labeled Sum of Identification Core Standard Scores in the Identification Chart on page 39 of the form. ❷ If the Identification Core composite is less than the cut score for the student's age, then the score is consistent with the presence of a language/literacy disorder. An example for the 8-year-old girl is shown in Figure 2.

Age Band	Sum of Identification Core Standard Scores	Cut Score	Sensitivity	Specificity
6–7 years		24	84	84
8–11 years	❶ 21	34	88	85
12–18 years		42	86	90

Decision:
Is the Identification Core composite less than the cut score?

X Yes
This score is consistent with the presence of a language/literacy disorder.

❷ ❒ No
This score is not consistent with the presence of a language/literacy disorder.

Figure 2. Identification Chart completed for an 8-year-old girl.

SUBTEST 11: **Reading Fluency (RF)**

Purpose: This subtest assesses the accuracy and automaticity of word-reading ability (i.e., without error, hesitation, repetition, or self-correction) in meaningful contexts.

Use as a stand-alone measure: Yes
Average time to administer: 2 minutes
Materials: *Examiner Record Form* (pp. 25–28), *Stimulus Book* (correct story for age), audio recording device (recommended)
Start rule:
- **Story A:** "The Class Pet" for ages 6;6–7;11 (p. 69)
- **Story B:** "The Principal's Daughter" for ages 8;0–10;11 (p. 71)
- **Story C:** "When the School Closed" for ages 11;0–13;11 (p. 73)
- **Story D:** "The Building" for ages 14;0–18;11 (p. 75)

Basal rule: None
Ceiling rule: If the student becomes upset or anxious, you may decide to discontinue. If so, count any unread words as 0.
Repetition: Not applicable
Probes: Yes (as specified in the *Examiner's Manual*)
Special instructions:
- ***Be sure*** to select the correct story for the student's age.
- ***You should*** tell an emergent reader, ***"Just read the words you know."***
- If the student experiences difficulty decoding words, say, ***"Just do your best."***

SUBTEST 12: **Written Expression (WE)**

Purpose: This subtest uses a sentence-combining task to assess a student's written expression skills at both the sound/word level and the sentence/discourse level. Students are asked to follow an example that shows how to rewrite short, simple sentences to sound less choppy and more interesting.

Use as a stand-alone measure: No (Subtest 11 must be administered immediately prior to Subtest 12 and in the same session.)
Average time to administer: 10 minutes
Materials: *Examiner Record Form* (pp. 29–31), *Stimulus Book* (p. 77; then correct story for age), *Student Response Form* (p. 8)
Start rule: Arrows with age ranges in years indicate which story to administer
- **Story A:** "The Class Pet" for ages 6;6–7;11 (p. 69)
- **Story B:** "The Principal's Daughter" for ages 8;0–10;11 (p. 71)
- **Story C:** "When the School Closed" for ages 11;0–13;11 (p. 73))
- **Story D:** "The Building" for ages 14;0–18;11 (p. 75)

Basal rule: None
Ceiling rule: If the student indicates being finished, record the time spent writing and move to the next subtest.
Repetition: Not applicable
Probes: Yes (as specified in the *Examiner's Manual*)

Special instructions:
- ***Refer to*** the *Examiner's Manual* (pp. 66–78) and the *Examiner's Practice Workbook* (pp. 86–104) for guidance on scoring content units and T-units.
- ***Be sure*** to select the correct story for the student's age.
- ***Do read*** the facts out loud for the student if the student had difficulty decoding the words during the Reading Fluency subtest.
- If you observe that the student is copying, you ***may say, "Remember that your job is not to copy the story. Your job is to use these facts and put them together in a way that sounds less choppy and more interesting."***
- If the student stops writing prematurely, you ***may say, "You still have some time to work on your story."***
- If a student works for 20 minutes without completing the task, you may say that it is time to stop.

SUBTEST 13: **Social Communication (SC)**

Purpose: This subtest assesses a student's ability to understand language describing social situations and to formulate responses that fit a social context, including tone of voice.

Use as a stand-alone measure: Yes
Average time to administer: 9 minutes
Materials: *Examiner Record Form* (pp. 32–35), *Stimulus Book* (pp. 80–107 for boys; pp. 108–135 for girls), audio recording device (recommended)
Start rule: Start points for age ranges are indicated by arrows
Basal rule: 6 consecutive item scores of 1
Ceiling rule: 6 scores of 0 out of 8 consecutive items

Repetition: Allowed
Probes: Yes (as specified in the *Examiner's Manual*)
Special instructions:
- ***You may*** remind the student to say it like the person in the scene would say it when coaching the practice item.
- ***You should*** use the probe, ***"Can you give me more?"*** if the student gives a one-word response.

SUBTEST 14: **Digit Span Forward (DSF)**

Purpose: This subtest assesses cognitive-linguistic skills required for auditory short-term (immediate) verbal memory with minimal demands on other aspects of language.

Use as a stand-alone measure: Yes
Average time to administer: 3 minutes
Materials: *Examiner Record Form* (p. 36)
Start rule: Start points for age ranges are indicated by arrows

Basal rule: Scores 1 on all items at any one level (a level is a set of items that all include the same number of digits and are shaded similarly)
Ceiling rule: Scores 0 on all items at any one level
Repetition: No (unless ambient noise interferes)
Probes: None

SUBTEST 15: **Digit Span Backward (DSB)**

Purpose: This subtest assesses verbal working memory in that the student must mentally manipulate the numbers heard in order to reproduce the digit names in reverse order.

Use as a stand-alone measure: No (Subtest 14 must be administered immediately prior to Subtest 15 and in the same session.)
Average time to administer: 3 minutes
Materials: *Examiner Record Form* (p. 37)
Start rule: Start points for age ranges are indicated by arrows

Basal rule: Scores 1 on all items at any one level
Ceiling rule: Scores 0 on all items at any one level
Repetition: No (unless ambient noise interferes)
Probes: None

SUBTEST 6: **Listening Comprehension (LC)**

Purpose: This subtest assesses a student's ability to comprehend the complex syntax of academic language and draw inferences allowed by the text as well as the metalinguistic knowledge to detect when a text does not provide sufficient information to answer certain questions definitively ("maybe").

Use as a stand-alone measure: Yes
Average time to administer: 7 minutes
Materials: *Examiner Record Form* (pp. 15–16)
Start rule: Start points for age ranges are indicated by arrows
Basal rule: All 3 items correct for 2 consecutive stories
Ceiling rule: All 3 items incorrect for 2 consecutive stories
Repetition: No (unless ambient noise interferes)

Probes: Yes (as specified in the *Examiner's Manual*)
Special instructions:

- During practice, you may say, ***"Could Teresa have a dog?"*** or ***"Are you sure Teresa does not have a dog (or has a dog)? The story didn't really tell us the answer, so you should say ____ [maybe]."***
- If the student indicates that he or she does not understand, say, ***"It's okay to take a guess."***

SUBTEST 7: **Reading Comprehension (RC)**

Purpose: This subtest assesses a student's ability to read and comprehend the complex syntax of academic language and draw inferences allowed by the text as well as the metalinguistic knowledge to detect when a text does not provide sufficient information to answer certain questions definitively ("maybe").

Use as a stand-alone measure: No (Subtest 6 must be administered immediately prior to Subtest 7 and in the same session.)
Average time to administer: 8 minutes
Materials: *Examiner Record Form* (pp. 17–18), *Student Response Form* (p. 3), pencil with eraser, cardstock (optional)
Start rule: Start points for age ranges are indicated by arrows (Do not administer to children age 6;0–6;5.)
Basal rule: All 3 items correct for 2 consecutive stories
Ceiling rule: All 3 items incorrect for 2 consecutive stories

Screening rule: Ask any student who might have a decoding problem to start by reading Story 1 aloud. If the student misreads seven or more words within the first story, discontinue testing, and write "emergent reader."
Repetition: Not applicable
Probes: Yes (as specified in the *Examiner's Manual*)
Special instructions:

- ***Do not*** assist the student to decode any words.
- ***You may*** point out any items that the student has neglected to answer throughout this subtest.

SUBTEST 8: **Following Directions (FD)**

Purpose: This subtest assesses a student's ability to listen to a sequence of directions, understand them, and hold them in short-term memory long enough to carry them out.

Use as a stand-alone measure: Yes
Average time to administer: 8 minutes
Materials: *Examiner Record Form* (pp. 19–20), *Student Response Form* (pp. 4–6), pencil with eraser, cardstock
Start rule: Start points for age ranges are indicated by arrows
Basal rule: 6 consecutive scores of 1
Ceiling rule: Scores 0 on 6 out of 8 consecutive items

Repetition: No (unless ambient noise interferes)
Probes: None
Special instructions:

- ***Do point out*** the importance of following the directions exactly when coaching the practice items.
- ***Do not forget*** to have the student cover up the stimuli while you give the spoken directions.

SUBTEST 9: **Delayed Story Retelling (DSR)**

Purpose: This subtest assesses retention and retelling of narrative discourse over a period of 20–30 minutes.

Use as a stand-alone measure: No (Subtest 9 must be administered 20–30 minutes following Subtest 3, with language-related activities intervening.)
Average time to administer: 2 minutes
Materials: *Examiner Record Form* (pp. 21–22), audio recording device (recommended)
Story A: "Tommy the Trickster" for ages 6;0–11;11 (p. 7 of the *Examiner Record Form*)
Story B: "The Rubber Raft" for ages 12;0–18;11 (p. 9 of the *Examiner Record Form*)

Start rule: Arrows with age ranges in years indicate which story to administer
Basal rule: None
Ceiling rule: None
Repetition: Not applicable
Probes: Yes (as specified in the *Examiner's Manual*)
Special instructions:

- ***You may*** prompt initiation by saying, ***"Just tell me anything you remember."***

SUBTEST 10: **Nonword Reading (NWRead)**

Purpose: This subtest assesses reading decoding by using nonwords that follow English orthographic rules to assess a student's ability to decode novel words that could not be memorized as real words.

Use as a stand-alone measure: Yes
Average time to administer: 4 minutes
Materials: *Examiner Record Form* (pp. 23–24), *Stimulus Book* (pp. 57–67), audio recording device (recommended)
Start rule: Start points for age ranges are indicated by arrows. (Do not administer to children age 6;0–6;5.)
Basal rule: 6 consecutive scores of 1
Ceiling rule: Scores 0 on 6 out of 8 consecutive items

Repetition: Not applicable
Probes: Yes (as specified in the *Examiner's Manual*)
Special instructions:

- ***You may*** prompt the student to ***"Give it a try."***
- ***You may*** ask, ***"So that word is ___?"*** to try to elicit a consolidated pronunciation if the student produces the word in separate chunks or individual sounds.

Using the TILLS for Purpose 2: To Document Patterns of Relative Strengths and Weaknesses

The Profile Chart generates a graphic presentation of the full range of sound/word level and sentence/discourse level skills across both the oral and written modalities. To create a TILLS profile, you should administer the complete set of TILLS subtests. Follow the steps outlined for the chart in Figure 3 to do the following. ❶ Enter the standard score from the front cover of the *Examiner Record Form* for each subtest. ❷ Mark an X over the corresponding score in the column. ❸ Draw a vertical line to connect the score to the mean (the horizontal line at 10 on the chart) for each subtest.

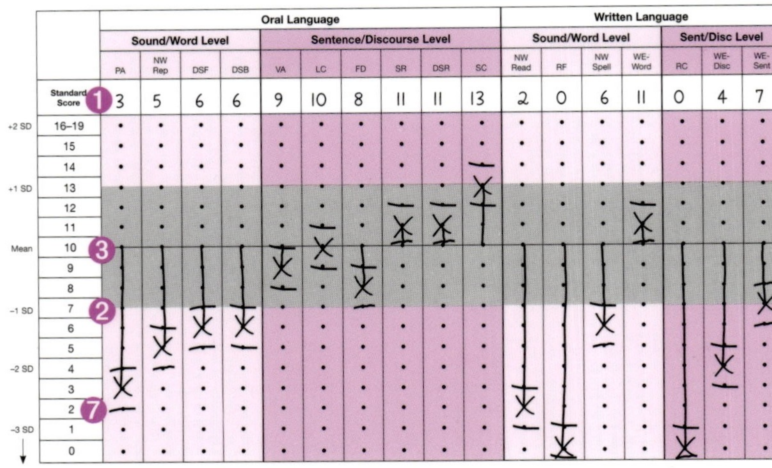

Figure 3. Profile Chart completed for an 8-year-old girl.

Completing and Using the Confidence Interval Tables

A student's true ability may be slightly higher or lower than the actual score received on the day of testing. You can use the confidence intervals around the actual scores to estimate the range of the student's true score (using 68% or 90% confidence intervals). To do this, follow Steps 4 through 7 on the back cover of the *Examiner Record Form.* For ❹ enter the subtest standard scores and the composite standard scores from page 1 into the appropriate cells in the confidence interval tables (see example in Figure 4). For ❺ decide whether to use the 68% or 90% confidence interval and look up the corresponding confidence interval values in the Appendix of the *Examiner's Manual.* For ❻ add and subtract these values from each of the standard scores and enter the resulting numbers in the appropriate upper and lower CI boxes. For ❼ draw short horizontal lines at these levels above and below the X that shows the student's standard score for each subtest. Use Steps 4 through 6 to find the confidence intervals for the composite scores as depicted in the small table in Figure 4.

	PA	NW Rep	DSF	DSB	VA	LC	FD	SR	DSR	SC	NW Read	RF	NW Spell	WE-Word	RC	WE-Disc	WE-Sent
❺ Upper CI value (+) for __% level 68%	4	6	7	7	10	11	9	12	12	14	3	2	7	12	1	5	8
Standard Score ❹	3	5	6	6	9	10	8	11	11	13	2	0	6	11	0	4	7
Lower CI value (-) for __% level 68% ❻	2	4	5	5	8	9	7	10	10	12	1	0	5	10	0	3	6

	TILLS Total	Sound/Word Composite	Sent/Disc Composite	Oral Composite	Written Composite	Identification Core
Upper CI value (+) for __% level 68%	70	61	85	87	59	68
Standard Score ❹	68	59	83	85	57	66
Lower CI value (-) for __% level 68% ❻	66	57	81	83	55	64

Figure 4. Tables used to calculate confidence intervals.

Using the TILLS for Purpose 3: To Track Changes in Language and Literacy Skills Over Time

To monitor language and literacy skill levels over time and relative to same age peers, the entire TILLS or selected subtests may be readministered after a minimum of 6 months. To use the Tracking Chart ❶, enter the Standard Scores obtained at Test Time 1 and at Test Time 2 in the appropriate column for each subtest administered. Then, subtract standard scores earned at Time 1 from scores earned at Time 2. Compare the absolute values ❷ of the difference (i.e., ignoring whether they are positive or negative) to the True Change Interval values ❸. (The values printed in the chart are for the 68% confidence interval; to use a 90% confidence interval, look up these values in the Appendix of the *Examiner's Manual.*) If the absolute value of the difference for a subtest is larger than the True Change Interval, enter "yes" (or Y) under Change Decision ❹. If not, enter "no" (or N). If yes, add a sign (+ or -) to indicate whether the difference is positive or negative or draw an arrow to indicate the direction of change as shown in Figure 5. See Chapter 3 of the *Examiner's Manual* for a caution in interpreting change across different age levels.

	Oral Language						Written Language					
	Sub-test	Standard Score Time 2	Standard Score Time 1	Difference	True Change Interval	Change Decision (yes/no)	Sub-test	Standard Score Time 2	Standard Score Time 1	Difference	True Change Interval	Change Decision (yes/no)
Sound/Word Level	PA	3	❶ 0	❷ +3	❸ 2	❹ Y↑	NW Read	2	1	+1	1	N
	NW Rep	5	4	+1	2	N	RF	0	0	0	2	N
	DSF	6	4	+2	2	N	NW Spell	6	8	-2	1	Y↓
	DSB	6	7	-1	2	N	WE-Word	11	10	+1	2	N
Sent/Disc Level	VA	9	7	+2	1	Y↑	RC	0	0	0	2	N
	LC	10	10	0	2	N	WE-Disc	4	4	0	1	N
	FD	8	8	0	2	N	WE-Sent	7	6	+1	1	N
	SR	11	10	+1	2	N						
	DSR	11	10	+1	2	N						
	SC	13	10	+3	2	Y↑						

Figure 5. Tracking Chart completed for an 8-year-old girl.

Visit www.brookespublishing.com/tills for more information on all components of the TILLS.

ISBN-13: 978-1-59857-914-7
ISBN-10: 1-59857-914-2

90000

9 781598 579147

PAUL H. BROOKES PUBLISHING CO.®
www.brookespublishing.com
Manufactured in the U.S.A.